CENGAGE Learning

Novels for Students, Volume 42

Project Editor: Sara Constantakis **Rights Acquisition and Management**: Christine Myaskovsky **Composition**: Evi Abou-El-Seoud **Manufacturing**: Rhonda Dover

Imaging: John Watkins

Product Design: Pamela A. E. Galbreath, Jennifer Wahi **Digital Content Production**: Allie Semperger **Product Manager**: Meggin Condino © 2013 Gale, Cengage Learning

For product information and technology assistance, contact us at **Gale Customer Support, 1-800-877-4253.**

For permission to use material from this text or product, submit all requests online at **www.cengage.com/permissions**.

Further permissions questions can be emailed to **permissionrequest@cengage.com** While every effort has been made to ensure the reliability of the information presented in this publication, Gale, a part of Cengage Learning, does not guarantee the accuracy of the data contained herein. Gale accepts no payment for listing; and inclusion in the publication of any organization, agency, institution, publication, service, or individual does not imply endorsement of the editors or publisher. Errors brought to the attention of the publisher and verified to the satisfaction of the publisher will be corrected in future editions.

Gale
27500 Drake Rd.
Farmington Hills, MI, 48331-3535

ISBN-13: 978-1-4144-9485-2
ISBN-10: 1-4144-9485-8
ISSN 1094-3552

This title is also available as an e-book.

ISBN-13: 978-1-4144-9271-1
ISBN-10: 1-4144-9271-5
Contact your Gale, a part of Cengage Learning sales representative for ordering information.

Printed in Mexico
1 2 3 4 5 6 7 17 16 15 14 13

Return to Sender

Julia Alvarez 2009

Introduction

Julia Alvarez's young-adult novel *Return to Sender* is one of several young-adult novels in which Alvarez features characters of Hispanic descent. In this novel, two families are brought together by the challenges faced by each family. Eleven-year-old Tyler Paquette's family is struggling to maintain the Vermont dairy farm that has been in their family for generations. The family has just suffered the loss of its patriarch, Tyler's grandfather. In addition, his father has been seriously injured in a farming accident, and Tyler's brother will soon be leaving for college. There is too much work for Tyler, his sister, and his mother to handle on their own.

However, the Paquettes soon decide that to save the farm, they will hire a family of Mexican immigrants to help them. Eleven-year-old Mari Cruz's family, which includes two younger sisters, her father, and two uncles, moves to Vermont from North Carolina. Mr. Cruz's brothers have been working in North Carolina illegally, and are soon joined by Mr. Cruz, his wife, and his daughter Mari. Mari's two younger sisters were born in the years following the family's arrival in North Carolina. As the novel begins, Mari's father and uncles have just been hired by Tyler's parents, and they profess to have the necessary paperwork to be working legally in the country, yet the Paquettes ask few questions. They need inexpensive laborers willing to work long hours, and the Cruzes need a place to live (the trailer on the Paquette farm) and a steady income, most of which gets sent back to their family in Mexico. The Cruzes are additionally coping with the fact that Mari's mother has not completed the return trip from Mexico following her recent departure to be with her dying mother.

As the story unfolds, the Cruzes and the Paquettes begin to overcome their suspicions and the biases they have toward one another. In particular, a close friendship develops between Tyler and Mari. Mari's mother eventually returns to the family after a horrifying ordeal, and Tyler plays a key role in reuniting her with her family. Despite the efforts of the Paquettes and the Cruzes working together to ensure that the Cruzes remain together and in Vermont, the novel concludes with Mari's family being deported, but reunited with their extended family in Mexico.

Return to Sender was published in 2009 by Yearling.

Author Biography

Born in New York City on March 27, 1950, Alvarez moved with her parents, native Dominicans, to the Dominican Republic not long after her birth. She spent the first ten years of her life in the Dominican Republic, but returned with her parents to the United States in 1960. Her family was forced to flee the Dominican Republic because of Alvarez's father's involvement in an unsuccessful rebellion against dictator Rafael Trujillo. After returning to New York, Alvarez's father, a doctor, established a medical practice and her mother stayed home to raise Alvarez and her three sisters. Alvarez was educated in boarding schools. She later attended Connecticut College for two years before transferring to Middlebury College in Vermont in 1969. She received a bachelor's degree in 1971, then pursued a master of fine arts degree from Syracuse University. Since completing the MFA program in 1975, Alvarez has held positions as Poet-in-the-Schools in Kentucky, Delaware, and North Carolina, from 1975 through 1978, and as a professor of creative writing and English at a number of institutions, including the University of Vermont and the University of Illinois. Alvarez published her first collection of poetry, *Homecoming: Poems*, in 1984. In 1989, Alvarez married Bill Eichner, a doctor and the father of two daughters. The marriage was Alvarez's third. Since 1988, Alvarez has held a professorship of English at

Middlebury College. She published her first novel, *How the García Girls Lost Their Accents*, in 1991. She has since published several other novels, including *In the Time of Butterflies* in 1995 and *Return to Sender* in 2009.

Chapter 1: Summer (2005)

In *Return to Sender*, each chapter is subdivided into two parts, the first being a titled section written from Tyler's point of view, and the second being a letter or series of letters written by Mari. In the first part of the first chapter, "Bad Luck Farm," Alvarez introduces the reader to Tyler Paquette and his family, who own a dairy farm in Vermont. Tyler's grandfather has recently died, and his father has been injured in a farming accident. The family is running the risk of losing the farm, which has been in the family for generations. Without Tyler's grandfather and his father, whose injuries prevent him from working as he used to, and with Tyler's brother going off to college, there are simply not enough able-bodied individuals to do the work that needs to be done. Tyler, his sister Sara, and their mother cannot handle all the work on their own, even with the help of their hired farm hand, Corey. Tyler reflects on his recent stay with his Aunt Roxie and Uncle Tony in Boston. His parents sent him to stay with them because they felt he needed a respite from his anxiety about the farm and his father. Upon his return, Tyler learns that his parents have hired three Mexican laborers to work on the farm. His parents have asked him to avoid discussing the newly hired men, or the daughters of one of the laborers.

Media Adaptations

- An unabridged audio recording of *Return to Sender*, read by Ozzie Rodriguez and Olivia Preciado, was published by Listening Library in 2010.

- The audio recording of *Return to Sender*, read by Ozzie Rodriguez and Olivia Preciado, is also available as an MP3 download, published by Audible.com in 2010.

The second part of the chapter consists of letters the daughter of one of the Mexican workers has written to her mother. The girl, Mari, indicates in her letters that she and her sisters, along with her father and uncles, have moved from North Carolina to Vermont to find more reliable work than what the men were able to secure in North Carolina. Mari was born in Mexico and entered the country illegally with her parents. Her uncles, also illegal immigrants, had already traveled to the United States and found work. Mari's two sisters, Ofie and Luby, were born in the United States. Mari's letters further reveal that Mari's mother has returned to Mexico to be with her dying mother. Although Mari's father received word that his wife had begun her return trip to the United States, she failed to arrive in North Carolina before the family moved to Vermont. Mari's father has been unable to find her or to retrace her steps.

Chapter 2: Summer into Fall (2005)

The first portion of this chapter is told from Tyler's point of view. His mother asks him to introduce himself to the Mexican girls who are now living in a trailer on the farm. The conversation is awkward, as Mari's sisters reveal that Mari, unlike them, was born in Mexico. Mari runs off crying, which confuses Tyler. Relating the incident to his parents at dinner, Tyler begins to understand that his parents are hiding something from him. Later that night, Tyler heads to the hayloft in the barn, a perch from which he enjoys setting up the telescope his grandfather gave him and looking out at the stars. Mari, however, is already there when he arrives. Although annoyed, Tyler softens when Mari expresses both an interest in and an aptitude for learning about the constellations. He is happy to be able to share his enthusiasm with someone else. When Tyler returns to the house, his parents discuss with him their concerns about the Mexican workers they have hired. As Mr. and Mrs. Paquette reveal, the Mexican workers have indicated that they are here legally, but Mr. and Mrs. Paquette have begun to suspect otherwise. Despite what they have told Tyler—that the Cruzes have assured the Paquettes that they have the proper documentation—the Paquettes' insistence on secrecy since the Cruzes' arrival suggests that Mr. and Mrs. Paquette have known since they hired the workers that they were most likely working in the United States illegally. Tyler is extremely concerned that his family is breaking the law. He asks his parents if they should call the police. In answer, his father asks him, "How badly do you want to stay on the farm, son?" Tyler does not answer, but feels as though he has suddenly entered a confusing grown-up world that makes no sense and has allowed him no access back to "that happier country of childhood."

In the next portion of the chapter, Mari writes a letter to the president. She explains that she is writing the letter as an assignment for school. In it, she details her story and attempts to demonstrate to the president the unfairness of immigration laws. She describes the way two boys on the school bus accused her of being in the country illegally, and how Tyler did little to defend her or to try and stop the boys from teasing her. She later confronts Tyler and asks if he is her friend. Tyler simply shrugs in reply. After Mari confronts him about what happened on the bus, Tyler asks if she has the documents she needs to be in the country legally. Mari does not lie to him, but tells him her family's story. She is disappointed by Tyler's response when he tells her that he understands that she has done nothing wrong, but that he would rather his family lose their farm than be disloyal to their country.

Chapter 3: Fall (2005)

In the section titled "Watched Over Farm," Tyler watches the night sky, believing that he sometimes sees his grandfather's face. From his bedroom window, he watches the comings and goings of Mari and her family, feeling guilty as he does so, but suspicious that they might be breaking the law. Tyler decides to approach his grandmother, hoping to ask her about how his grandfather would have felt about the illegal Mexicans working for them. He is surprised to find out that she is becoming quite close with the Cruz girls, and that they have shared with her stories about the Mexican holiday known as the Day of the Dead. Tyler's grandmother is comforted by the idea of creating an altar for her deceased husband, and she plans on celebrating the Day of the Dead by inviting the girls over to dinner. She asks Tyler to join them. The two then converse about Tyler's grandfather, and Tyler confesses everything that he has been thinking and feeling regarding his grandfather's death and Tyler's conviction that his grandfather is visiting him in the night sky. The Day of the Dead dinner allows Tyler and Mari the opportunity to reconnect. Believing, after his conversation with his grandmother, that his grandfather would have approved of the family allowing the Cruzes a chance to earn a leaving, Tyler is eager to renew his friendship with the girls.

The chapter then shifts to Mari's perspective, captured in a letter she writes to her dead grandmother as an assignment for her Day of the Dead unit at school. In this letter, Mari recounts the Day of the Dead celebrations with her American grandmother (Tyler's grandmother, who has asked the girls to call her "Grandma") and with her own family. Mari expresses the devastation she felt when her sister Ofie placed the portrait of their mother alongside that of Abuelita (the children's grandmother) as part of the ceremony. Her father and her sisters seem to accept that the girls' mother is not returning, but Mari refuses to come to this conclusion. Not long afterward, Mr. Cruz calls their old home phone number in North Carolina, to see how their acquaintances from Mexico were coming along. Finding the number disconnected, Mr. Cruz calls another friend, still working in North Carolina, who confirms that the home had been raided, their acquaintances had been deported, and that the apartment had been taken over by other Mexicans. Mari and Mr. Cruz begin to worry that in the event María Antonia Santos (Mari's mother) did return to the apartment; she would not know where her family had moved. Mari grabs the phone and begs the friend to go to the apartment and tell the new tenants the Cruzes' phone number, should María return there. The family is very shaken, and when trick-or-treaters knock on the door, the Cruzes do not answer. Tyler's mother, Connie, comes to check on the family after seeing that the trailer had been splattered with eggs and rotten fruit. She brings Halloween candy for the children. Mari closes the letter to her deceased grandmother on a note of deep sadness and fear for her mother's safety.

Chapter 4: Late Fall (2005)

The first section of chapter four, "Farm of Many Plots," opens with Thanksgiving at Grandma Paquette's house. She has invited all of her children and their families, as well as the Cruz family. Despite some initial awkwardness between the Paquettes' extended family and the Mexican laborers, the day progresses smoothly, until Mari overhears Uncle Larry and Mr. Paquette discussing the Homeland Security Department's increased efforts to track down illegal aliens in the area. While Tyler attempts to help the girls come up with an escape plan, Aunt Jeanne tries to convince her siblings that Grandma Paquette needs to move in with one of her children or move to a nursing home. Jeanne fears for her mother's safety after having overheard her talking to her dead husband, and after the elderly Mrs. Paquette was involved in several minor traffic accidents. Meanwhile, Sara answers the phone. She believes her former boyfriend has been calling and hanging up, and she threatens to call the police, but the Cruz girls wonder if it is their mother calling in search of them. When the phone rings again, Mari answers, but it is in fact Sara's old boyfriend. Sara and Tyler are confused, and do not understand how the girls cannot know where their mother is.

The second section of the chapter takes the form of Mari's letter written to the Virgin of Guadalupe on her Catholic feast day. Through this letter, the reader learns that Mari's uncle, Tío Filipe, is being sought by Homeland Security officers. Mari explains that Filipe, who is close in age to Tyler's older brother Ben, was invited by Ben to attend a party. On the way home, Ben was speeding and was pulled over. When the officer directed his flashlight into the vehicle and spotted Filipe, Filipe became frightened of being apprehended, and he fled. The remaining Cruzes are fearful that the police will come for them. Hiding out in their trailer, they are surprised by the appearance of Tyler's grandmother. She informs them of her family's plan to put her in a nursing home if she does not agree to move in with one of them. The Cruzes are horrified that she would be treated this way by her own children, and allow her to stay with them until the evening, when her friend will pick her up. Tyler's mother arrives but Mr. Cruz does not let her in. As they converse through the door, Mrs. Paquette informs them that Filipe had been caught in another county, but because he had fled from he police, he would have to stand trial, rather than just have a hearing and be deported. The next day, Tyler's Aunt Jeanne and Uncle Bryon approach the trailer and ask if the Cruzes know anything about Grandma Paquette. Seeing how worried Jeanne is about her mother, Armando makes Jeanne promise not to send Grandma away, then tells her where

Grandma may be found. Tyler returns home from school to find the family reunited. Mari closes the letter by praying that her family will be reunited as well.

Chapter 5: Winter (2005–2006)

The fifth chapter opens with the section "Christmas Tears Farms." Tyler is worried about Filipe Cruz and about the family's first Christmas without his grandfather. The Cruz and Paquette families learn that Filipe will have to go through a criminal trial, and possibly serve time, before going through a deportation hearing. The Paquettes find a lawyer from an organization in Burlington, Vermont. These lawyers donate their time and take on cases like Filipe's for free. Tyler comes up with the idea of asking their Spanish teacher, Mrs. Ramirez, to accompany Mrs. Paquette and the lawyer when they visit Filipe in jail. She agrees. In the meantime, Tyler helps Mr. Cruz purchase gifts for the three girls for Christmas, as none of the Cruzes is leaving the farm for fear of being captured. He also purchases presents for the girls himself, considering carefully what to get for Mari. Tyler accompanies Mrs. Paquette, the lawyer Caleb Calhoun, and Mrs. Ramirez when they visit Filipe. Fulfilling Mari's Christmas wish, Tyler "delivers" her letter to Filipe by allowing him to read the letter through the bullet-proof glass that separates the prisoners from their visitors. Later, when the phone rings at the Paquette house, Sara urgently tells Tyler to bring one of the Cruzes to the phone, as she believes it is their mother calling, but as Mari later writes in a letter, the caller hung up by the time Mari's father got to the phone.

In the next section of the chapter, Mari writes to her uncle, Filipe. Through these letters, Mari explains how the Paquette family is trying to help Felipe and how they have spent the holidays together. Mari's letters also reveal that Filipe will serve no additional time on criminal charges and that he has been handed over to the Homeland Security officers to await his deportation hearing. A later letter indicates that Filipe will finally be returning to Mexico. Mari also explains that her father is growing increasingly strict with the girls about how they spend their time and is insisting that they speak only Spanish in the home. Mari believes he is trying to prepare them in case they have to abruptly return to Mexico.

Chapter 6: And More Winter (2006)

In the first section of the sixth chapter, "Farm for the Lost & Found," Tyler and his family and Mari attend a town meeting in which Tyler is asked to carry in the flag and recite the Pledge of Allegiance. Before the meeting begins, Tyler finds a large sum of money in the bathroom. He knows he should find its owner, but he is tempted to keep the money. His 4H Club is going to Washington, D.C., but Tyler's family cannot afford for Tyler to go, even though it is what he wants more than anything for his upcoming birthday, which is the next day. Pocketing the money for now, Tyler performs his duties and then takes a seat for the meeting. During the meeting, an elderly man makes an announcement that the laws against hiring illegal workers should be enforced, and he advocates arresting anyone who has hired them and sending the illegal workers back to their home country. Tyler's teacher, Mr. Bicknell, points out that the United States was built on a foundation of immigrant labor, and draws attention to the Italian immigrant ancestry of Mr. Rossetti's own family. After Mr. Rossetti's motion is voted down and the meeting adjourns, the citizens of the town file out of the building. Mr. Rossetti suddenly runs from the building, shouting that he has been robbed. Overcome with emotion, Mr. Rossetti collapses. He is caught by his neighbors, at which point Tyler quietly returns the money to Mr. Rossetti.

The next section of the chapter consists once again of Mari's letters. She writes to her family back in Mexico, telling them how glad she is that her uncle Filipe returned safely. She also describes for them Tyler's birthday party and tells them about Tyler's brother Ben's friend, Alyssa, who will be visiting a town in Mexico to volunteer at a clinic there. The town is not far from Mari's family's village, and Mari informs her uncle that Alyssa will bring to Filipe his beloved guitar. Mari tells them about the phone calls the Paquettes have been receiving, and their concerns about Mari's mother. Mari's letter also describes an incident at school, in which, on Valentine's Day, Mr. Bicknell asked the students to write about different kinds of love. Mari wrote about how the Paquette family has become good friends with her own. Because she mentions Tyler specifically, and how he has taught her about astronomy, the other children in the class tease both Mari and Tyler about being in love. Tyler becomes angry, claiming that Mari could get his family in trouble, but his reaction also stems from his embarrassment about being teased. Mari explains how the tension between the two of them eased, particularly after the town meeting in which Tyler began to realize the risks Mari's family ran in helping his. She describes the way Tyler is working for Mr. Rossetti around his house, trying to raise extra money so that he can go on the trip to Washington. This lengthy letter also explains that Tyler's grandmother is tasked with picking up Tyler from Mr. Rossetti's, and that Mari and her sisters often go with her. In this manner, a new friendship has formed, in which the girls refer to Mr. Rossetti as Grandpa, and Grandma Paquette develops her own friendship with Mr. Rossetti.

Chapter 7: Almost Spring (2006)

This chapter opens with the section "Interrobang Farm." Mari and Tyler learn about the punctuation mark known as the interrobang, in which a question mark and exclamation point are used together at the end of a sentence. Tyler learns that Mr. Cruz has asked his parents for money and time off. He has discovered that his wife is being held by smugglers in Texas who are demanding a large sum of money for him to ransom her from them. Grandma Paquette asks to borrow money from Mr. Rossetti to lend to Mr. Cruz, but Mr. Rossetti is resistant. Mari tells Tyler and Grandma Paquette that the men who have their mother have lowered their asking price by half, and that her father and her uncles in California have come up with the money. Again, the situation with Mari's mother changes, as her captors announce that for an additional $500, they will deliver Mari's mother to North Carolina rather than simply dropping her off in a Texas border town. Tyler, who has managed to save the same amount of money to go to Washington with his club (although the trip has been postponed due to protests in Washington over immigration laws), insists on the Cruzes taking the money. When Tyler's aunt and uncle call and apologize for missing his birthday, they offer to take him and friends of his choosing on a trip. He asks them to take him to North Carolina instead of Washington and devises a plan for rescuing Mari's mother.

The second part of the chapter consists of Mari's letter to her father. Mari and Sara have accompanied Tyler on his trip with his aunt and uncle. He has explained to Aunt Roxie and Uncle Tony that they need to go to Durham, North Carolina, to pick up Mari's mother, but Tyler has left out important details about Mari's mother and her status as an illegal immigrant for whom they are paying ransom to release her from her captors. Mari explains to her father that her mother's condition is seriously altered. Not only is she extremely thin, but she appears to have been beaten. She is timid, fearful, jumpy, and cries out at night in her sleep. Mari tells her father that, according to her mother, she was abducted by men referred to as coyotes. These men intercept illegal immigrants coming into the United States from Mexico and hold them for ransom from the families already living in the United States. Mari's mother was not treated well and was forced to live in the home of one of the men as his "servant," as she hesitantly describes it. Mari goes on to tell her father the way Tyler's aunt and uncle continued to help her mother, buying her new clothes to wear and helping her to feel as comfortable as possible. Mari ends her letter by expressing her excitement that they will soon be on their way home to Vermont after a stop in Washington, D.C.

Chapter 8: Spring (2006)

The section "Return-to-Sender Farm" opens this chapter. In it, Tyler reveals that, despite the fact that Mari's mother has returned, all is not well with Mari's family. Her mother seems extremely traumatized by her experiences. Their parents talk privately and weep openly, and Mari's mother still wakes up screaming. On Mother's Day, Grandma announces that she will be going with her church group to visit the town in Mexico where Alyssa went. Mr. Rossetti does not want her to go, but insists that he will come with her. The gathered families also celebrate Mari's birthday, which is the next day. Tyler finds a website from which a person can name a star for someone, and he decides to do this for Mari for her birthday. When he visits her at the trailer to give her the certificate about the star, he senses tension within the home. She does not invite him in, but Mari is allowed to sit on the steps and talk to Tyler. Mari's father has grown increasingly wary of Tyler's presence. Additionally, Mari informs Tyler that her father is preparing the family to move back to Mexico, as he has just seen announced on television the government's plan to build a wall along the U.S.-Mexican border. Later, at Tyler's grandmother's house, Tyler and Mari and her sisters are helping Grandma Paquette and Mr. Rossetti prepare flags to be placed at the graves of veterans for Memorial Day. Tyler takes the opportunity to show Mari her star with his telescope. However, they soon spot several cars with flashing lights approaching the farm.

The next section of the chapter consists of Mari's letter to the diary she received from her mother for her birthday. She describes the way officers went to the trailer and took away her father, mother, and uncle, while she and her sisters were at Grandma Paquette's house. Grandma Paquette takes the girls to Mr. Rossetti's house to hide. As Mari's description of events unfolds, she reveals that her father has been taken to a detention center in New York, and her mother has been taken elsewhere. She has been connected with the men who held her captive, for the men had Mari's mother's documents as well as phone numbers that connected her to Vermont. Mari tells Mrs. Ramirez, who has been helping the Paquettes as a translator in the process of securing information about the Cruzes, that she would like to talk to the Immigration and Custom Enforcement officers and tell them her family's story. She thinks perhaps it will help them be able to return to Mexico as a family, rather than being separated if her parents have to serve prison sentences. Mrs. Ramirez agrees and arranges the meeting.

On the way to the meeting, Mr. Calhoun explains that Mari's parents were seized in a government operation called Operation Return to Sender, which targeted illegal immigrants with a criminal record, such as the smugglers who abducted Mari's mother. Once they were captured, the paper trail led the government agents to the Cruzes. Mari tells her family's story to the government agent, Mr. O'Goody, who expresses his sympathy. Through Mr. O'Goody's efforts, Mari's family will be returned to Mexico, where her Uncle Armando has already been sent, in return for Mari's mother's testimony against the smugglers. Tyler is devastated to learn that his friend and her family must leave.

Chapter 9: Summer Again (2006)

The final chapter of the book begins with Tyler's letter to Mari, who is staying in Boston with her family at Tyler's aunt and uncle's house until their deportation is arranged. Tyler explains that his parents have decided to sell the farm, but to Tyler's Uncle Larry, who owns the neighboring farm, and who will sell it back to Tyler's family if and when they are one day ready. Tyler also expresses how much Mari's friendship means to him.

The chapter continues with another letter, this one from Mari to Tyler. She and her family are now in Mexico and are preparing to say goodbye to Grandma Paquette and Mr. Rossetti, who have come with their church group. She talks about how her parents are becoming more and more like their old selves once again. Mari also tells Tyler that when Ofie is eighteen years old, she will be able to return to America on her own as a citizen and sponsor their parents and Mari, who will at that time be able to attempt to apply for citizenship. Although Mari misses Vermont and school and Tyler, she also recognizes how happy being in Mexico makes her parents, and how grateful her extended family is for their return.

Alyssa

Alyssa is a friend of Ben Paquette's who becomes involved with Filipe Cruz. She volunteers at a medical clinic in Mexico during her spring break and brings Filipe his guitar. She also helps to serve as a go-between for members of the Cruz family in Mexico and Vermont.

Mr. Bicknell

Mr. Bicknell is Mari's and Tyler's teacher. He makes an effort to incorporate lessons into the classroom designed to educate the students about Mexican culture and immigration issues. He also defends immigrants at a town meeting.

Uncle Byron

Uncle Byron is Aunt Jeanne's husband and Tyler's uncle. A professor, he appears distant from the rest of his wife's family and remains in another room reading the *New York Times* while the family discusses the likely fate of the immigrant workers as well as Grandma Paquette's well-being. When his wife, Jeanne, becomes distraught after Grandma Paquette disappears, he is able to converse with the Cruzes in Spanish and ask for their help in finding her.

Caleb Calhoun

Caleb Calhoun is a lawyer who works for free on behalf of the Cruz family. Mrs. Paquette arranges for him to meet with Filipe after he is arrested, and he advises the Cruzes and the Paquettes in the cases against Mari's parents as well.

Corey

Corey is a farm hand who works for the Paquettes. He is mentioned at the beginning of the novel as being employed by the Paquettes. Corey is unable to work the long hours the farm requires. He does not appear in the novel and is not mentioned after the Cruzes' arrival.

Armando Cruz

Armando Cruz is Mari's older uncle, or Tío Armando. He is quieter than his brothers, and when he is arrested by Immigration and Custom Enforcement officers, he goes quietly, unlike his brother (Mari's father). Armando is deported without delay.

Filipe Cruz

Filipe Cruz is Mari's uncle, or Tío Filipe. He is the youngest of the Cruz brothers and described as being close to Tyler's brother Ben's age. Invited by

Ben to a party, Filipe is with him when Ben is pulled over for speeding on the way home from the party. He becomes nervous when the police approach the vehicle and he flees on foot. He is captured not long after, and the Cruzes consider him a hero, as he fled as far from the Paquette farm as he could before being apprehended. He is deported, but not before sparking the romantic interest of Alyssa.

Luby Cruz

María Loubyneida, or Luby, is the youngest of the Cruz daughters. Born in North Carolina like her sister Ofie, Luby is an American citizen. She is depicted as loving and sweet and sparks in members of the Paquette family a desire to protect her and her sisters.

Mari Cruz

María Dolores, or Mari, is the oldest of the Cruz daughters; she is eleven years old when the novel opens. The reader is first introduced to Mari in her letter to her long-absent mother. Mari's fearfulness about her mother's safety and her longing for her return are the most prominent features of her character through much of the novel. As the oldest, Mari is relied upon heavily by her father. She helps him communicate with Americans, and she helps care for her little sisters in their mother's absence. Mari is deeply touched by the unfairness of the world around her. Unlike her sisters, she was born in Mexico, and has a greater understanding of her family's roots there. At the same time, she does not understand why she and her family are regarded as criminals by the government and so many others. Mari thrives in school and is always eager to learn, as when Tyler teaches her about the constellations. As the novel progresses, Mari becomes increasingly close to Tyler and increasingly connected to Vermont and is always fearful that her family will be deported. When Mari's mother is finally rescued and reunited with her family, Mari is frightened by the changes in her mother and can only imagine what she endured, as her mother has only told her a fraction of her experiences. Once the family has been returned to Mexico, Mari focuses on the connections that she hopes will continue to tie her family with Tyler's and with the United States.

Mr. Cruz

Mr. Cruz is the father of Mari, Ofie, and Mari and the husband of María Santos. He attempts to keep his family safe and united. The job on the Paquette farm in Vermont appeals to him because his family can remain together. In North Carolina, he is forced to leave his family for weeks at a time to find work. A strict but loving father, Mr. Cruz relies heavily on Mari, who often serves as his translator and who must help take care of her sisters. Through Mari's observations about her father, Mr. Cruz is revealed to be distraught over his wife's disappearance and fearful about her fate and that of the rest of the family. After María's rescue,

Mr. Cruz becomes even more protective of his daughters and more suspicious of outsiders. After the family is deported, Mr. Cruz seems relieved to be back in Mexico and becomes politically active in his town.

Ofie Cruz

María Ofelia, or Ofie, is the middle daughter in the Cruz family. Unlike her older sister Mari, Ofie is outspoken and confident. Aware of her American citizenship, Ofie, perhaps more than her sisters, is eager to live as an American, and is reluctant to speak Spanish at home. She is resistant to the idea of returning to Mexico. She is often in conflict with Mari. After returning to Mexico with her family, Ofie plans to go back to America when she is eighteen and sponsor the citizenship applications of her family members.

Aunt Jeanne

Aunt Jeanne is Mr. Paquette's sister and Uncle Byron's wife. Her role in the story is small. She attempts to convince her siblings that their mother, Tyler's Grandma Paquette, is incapable of living on her own and needs to move in with one of her children or enter a nursing home. Ultimately, Jeanne loses this battle. After her mother's disappearance, she begs the Cruzes for help in finding Grandma Paquette.

Roxanne Mahoney

Roxanne Mahoney is Tyler's Aunt Roxie. She is Connie Paquette's sister and Tony Mahoney's wife. Perceived by her sister Connie to be free-spirited, Roxanne and her husband make a generous gift to Tyler after they miss his birthday, offering to take Tyler and his friends on a trip to Washington, D.C. Tyler asks them instead to go North Carolina, where they assist Tyler in the rescue of Mari's mother.

Tony Mahoney

Tony Mahoney is Roxanne's husband, and Tyler's uncle. Along with his wife, Tony aids in rescuing Mari's mother from her captors.

Mr. O'Goody

Mr. O'Goody is the Immigration and Custom Enforcement agent who is assigned to Mari's parents' cases. He listens with sympathy to Mari's story and is instrumental in expediting the Cruzes' deportation and helping the Cruzes avoid criminal prosecutions.

Ben Paquette

Ben Paquette is the oldest child of Connie Paquette and Mr. Paquette. As the story opens, Ben is preparing to leave home to attend college. During the course of the novel, Ben becomes friends with

Filipe Cruz and invites him to attend a party with him. When Ben is pulled over for speeding on the way home from the party, Filipe flees the vehicle, certain he will be discovered as an illegal immigrant. Ben feels responsible for Filipe's subsequent arrest and deportation.

Connie Paquette

Connie Paquette is Tyler, Ben, and Sara's mother and the wife of Mr. Paquette. She is depicted as a loving, if overprotective, mother. After Mr. Paquette's injury, she advises her husband to sell the farm. Nevertheless, she supports her husband's decision to hire immigrant workers, but she is surprised to find that three little girls are part of the arrangement. She is friendly and kind toward them and encourages her children to behave in a similar manner. When Filipe is arrested, Mrs. Paquette finds free legal council (Mr. Calhoun) and persistently works as an advocate for the fair treatment of the Cruz family after Armando and Mari's parents are arrested. Although she frequently embarrasses her son, Mrs. Paquette is revealed to be compassionate and understanding.

Elsie Paquette

See Grandma Paquette

Grandma Paquette

Grandma Paquette is Mr. Paquette's mother

and grandmother to Tyler, Sara, and Ben. Although devastated by her husband's recent death, Grandma Paquette finds renewed purpose in caring for the Cruz girls, who visit her after school to keep her company. Of all the Paquettes, she is the most welcoming to the Cruz family and invites them to holiday meals. Grandma Paquette helps Tyler to understand that his grandfather would have not wanted him to shun the Cruzes due to their illegal status. This approval transforms Tyler and his relationship with Mari. Throughout the novel, Grandma Paquette grows increasingly invested in the Cruz family, and shelters the three girls after their uncles and parents have been arrested. Moved by all she has learned of the Cruzes' culture, she follows the lead of Alyssa (Ben's friend who has become romantically interested in Filipe) and plans a trip to a village in Mexico to volunteer there. Grandma Paquette additionally transforms Mr. Rossetti's views regarding the illegal immigrants, as her relationship with him develops. Mr. Rossetti is the only character in the novel to call Grandma Paquette by her given name, Elsie.

Gramps Paquette

The grandfather of Tyler, Sara, and Ben, the father of Mr. Paquette, and the husband of Grandma Paquette, Gramps dies before the novel begins. Yet his death has an enormous impact on Tyler in particular, who was extremely close to his grandfather. As Tyler's father's accident occurred not long after Gramps's death, Tyler has grown fearful about his father's own mortality. During his life, Gramps shared his love of astronomy with Tyler, and it is through the stars that Tyler feels he remains connected with his grandfather.

Larry Paquette

Larry Paquette is the brother of Mr. Paquette, and Tyler's uncle. He owns the adjoining farm and employs his own illegal immigrant workers. He warns his brother that the authorities are beginning to be less tolerant of illegal workers, and he suspects that the Paquettes are in danger of losing their workforce. After Tyler's father's farm is raided, Larry, who manages to avoid the scrutiny of Homeland Security and Immigration and Customs Enforcement agents, helps his brother by buying Mr. Paquette's dairy farm and maintaining it should Mr. Paquette or his children want to buy it back.

Mr. Paquette

Mr. Paquette is the father of Tyler, Sara, and Ben, and the husband of Connie. Mr. Paquette owns a family dairy farm in Vermont. Before the story opens, he has been injured in a farm accident, being partially crushed by his tractor when it flips over on him. Tyler's quick thinking saved his father's life, but Mr. Paquette is unable to work the farm as he attempts to rehabilitate his damaged leg, arm, and hand. Fearful of losing the farm and reluctant to give in to his wife's gentle prodding that they sell, Mr. Paquette takes his brother Larry's approach and hires Mexican immigrant workers. He claims to have believed that they were in the country legally, but the secrecy with which he treats their arrival suggests otherwise. As he attempts to explains to his son, obeying the laws of your country is important, but when the laws need changing, and when you are trying to protect your way of living, your livelihood, and your family, disobeying the law is sometimes your only choice. As the story progresses, Mr. Paquette eventually regains some of his former mobility and is able to help on the farm. After the Cruz family is deported, he decides to sell his farm to his brother.

Sara Paquette

Sara Paquette is the middle child in the Paquette family. Tyler and Ben's sister and the daughter of Mr. and Mrs. Paquette, Sara is often regarded as vain and annoying from Tyler's point of view. Yet she becomes increasingly influenced by the Cruz family and becomes open to new ideas. She accompanies Aunt Roxie, Uncle Tony, Tyler, and Mari on the trip to rescue Mari's mother.

Tyler Paquette

Tyler Paquette, is, along with Mari, one of the main characters in the novel. Not long after Tyler's grandfather dies, his father is injured in a farm accident that Tyler saw happen. Because Tyler remained calm and called an ambulance, his father survived the accident. Tyler is distraught about the possibility of losing the farm when the novel opens, and he is consequently sent stay with his Aunt Roxie and Uncle Tony in Boston. Upon his return, he finds that his parents have hired immigrant laborers to help work the farm. Tyler gradually becomes friends with the children, particularly Mari, who is the same age as Tyler. But when he finds out that she and her family are working in the United States illegally, Tyler pulls away. He spies on them and worries that his parents are breaking the law. At the same time, he feels guilty for acting as though the Cruzes are criminals. After speaking with his grandmother, Tyler becomes reassured that his grandfather would have understood that some laws are unfair, and that everybody deserves the right to work and provide for their family. This understanding compels Tyler to reach out once again to Mari. As his friendship with her deepens, so does his understanding of what her family has been going through. Tyler becomes instrumental in securing the freedom of Mari's mother. He offers the Cruzes the hundreds of dollars he has saved and arranges with his aunt and uncle the trip to North Carolina to retrieve Mari's mother. Tyler's willingness to take such risks for Mari's family and the thoughtfulness of his gift to her—he has a star named after her—underscore the changes he experiences in the novel as well as the depth of his feelings for Mari.

Vicky Paquette

Vicky Paquette is Larry Paquette's wife and

Tyler's aunt. She does not play a large role in the story, but is depicted as concerned about the Cruz family, about the immigrants she and her husband employ, and about her family's ability to maintain their own farm.

Mrs. Ramirez

Mrs. Ramirez is the Spanish teacher at Tyler and Mari's school. Tyler asks her to serve as a translator when Filipe is arrested, and she further aids the Paquettes and the Cruzes after Mari's parents and Uncle Armando are taken into custody by Immigration and Custom Enforcement officers.

Joseph Rossetti

Joseph Rossetti is first introduced at a town meeting at which he suggests that illegal immigrants be tracked down and deported. Later, however, his views change after he becomes involved with Grandma Paquette and the Cruzes.

María Antonio Santos

María Antonio Santos is the mother of Mari, Luby, and Ofie Cruz and the wife of Mr. Cruz. She is present through much of the novel as a memory. In the beginning of the novel, Mari reveals through letters that her mother had left their home in North Carolina to return to Mexico when her mother was dying. Her journey back to the United States involved the assistance of relatives in California.

Along the way she was supposed to be posing as the wife of a Native American and reentering the country via a Native American reservation. Instead, she was captured and taken prisoner by men who smuggle Mexicans in and out of the country for a fee. They held María against her will and, after locating her family, sought a ransom for her release. When Tyler and the Cruzes rescue María, it is clear that she has endured much, and there are things she will not speak of to Mari. Only after María and her family are deported and settled in Mexico does María begin to recover from her ordeal.

Themes

Family

In *Return to Sender*, Alvarez presents two families with distinctly different cultural backgrounds and explores the relationship that develops between the two groups. The Cruzes and the Paquettes each have their own traditions as well as tensions. Mari's family is coping with the fact that they have no way of uncovering what has happened to Mari's mother. They run the constant risk of being discovered as illegal immigrants and returned to Mexico. Mari's greatest fear throughout the novel is that her family will never be together again, and in fact, her family is repeatedly fractured as the story progresses. Her mother's absence is prolonged. Her Uncle Filipe is arrested and deported. Not long after her mother's return, Mari and her sisters become separated from their mother, father, and other uncle, as the adults are all taken away by Immigration and Customs Enforcement officers. Further, it pains Mari to know that these three adults are all separated from one another: Armando is deported quickly, while her parents are held separately on various criminal charges.

Tyler's family likewise experiences separations. Gramps has recently died, and Ben is leaving for school. Tyler feels extremely isolated as he contemplates the possible loss of the farm.

Internally, the Paquette family is rife with tension as well, not only regarding the farm and its newly hired illegal immigrants, but over the issue of Grandma Paquette as well. As Grandma Paquette draws on cultural traditions regarding death from the Cruz girls, she incorporates the notion of a Day of the Dead altar to Gramps as a way of keeping him close and his memory alive. She speaks to him as if he were present. While these things help her cope with the loss of her husband, they, along with a few minor car accidents, indicate to her children that she should not be living alone. Her daughter Jeanne presses her siblings to force their mother to either agree to live with one of them or to be put in a nursing home. When the Cruz family hears of this, they are astonished and angered that an elderly person would be treated with so little dignity; it contradicts their own traditions and attitudes toward elderly family members, who are treated with the utmost consideration and respect. Through the Cruzes' advocacy, Grandma is spared the fate of being forced to move from her home, and the Paquettes learn a deeper respect for their eldest family member. Similarly, Grandma's welcoming of the Cruzes into the Paquettes' lives and homes encourages in both families a broader notion of what family means. Both families aid in the continued assurance of livelihood for the other. Further, both families work to keep the other family intact, as the Cruzes help repair the rift between Grandma and the rest of the family, and the Paquettes help secure the safe return of Mari's mother.

Topics for Further Study

- *A Step from Heaven* is a young-adult novel by the Korean-born An Na. In this 2002 novel, four-year-old Young Ju moves from Korea to California with her family. The novel centers on her childhood and adolescence and the challenges she faces as an immigrant. Read *A Step from Heaven* with a small group. Create an online blog that will serve as your book discussion forum. Consider the ways in which the experiences of Young Ju and Mari from Alvarez's *Return to Sender* are similar. Do they experience discrimination or teasing? How do their families fit in with their communities? What internal stresses do the families face? How successful are the authors in communicating the struggles of their protagonists? As you discuss the novels, consider as well the structure of each work, and compare Alvarez's use of letters to An Na's incorporation of short-story-like chapters.

- In *Return to Sender*, Alvarez explores the relationships that develop between a family of migrant farm workers from Mexico and a family of Vermont dairy farmers. The two protagonists are not yet teenagers but are beginning to experience the complexities of the adult world. Similarly, in Thanhha Lai's 2011 *Inside Out and Back Again*, a ten-year-old Vietnamese protagonist flees with her family to the United States during the Vietnam War. A story told in a series of free-verse poems, Lai's book is based on her own experiences attempting to assimilate in the United States as a child refugee. Her experiences of isolation mirror those of Mari. Read Lai's novel and create a report on the work in which you examine its plot, characters, and themes. Your report may be an essay or a visual time-line and summary created as a poster board or as an electronic presentation (with PowerPoint or on a web page you create).

- The bulk of Alvarez's novel is set on a dairy farm in Vermont. Using print and online sources, research the history of dairy farming in Vermont. Explore the twenty-first-century decline in family farms and discuss the evolution of larger-scale commercial dairy farms. Consider the way dairy farmers have incorporated migrant workers into their everyday operations. Prepare a written report or publish your work as a web page. Be sure to cite all of your sources.

- In *Return to Sender*, Alvarez makes reference to the 2006 series of government raids targeting illegal immigrants that was known as Operation Return to Sender. Research this operation and discuss its role in the immigration policies of the Bush administration. Use online news sources to help guide your research efforts. Prepare a presentation or a written report in which you provide a summary of Operation Return to Sender, its aims, and the consequences of the operation for illegal immigrants and their families.

Adolescence

Through the characters of Mari and Tyler, Alvarez explores the theme of adolescence. Both Mari and Tyler begin the book as eleven-year-olds. They are both twelve by the novel's end. Throughout this period, they are both forced to confront difficult adult realities and learn how to cope with new, unfamiliar, and morally complex situations. Mari is put in a position, initiated by her mother's absence, of being responsible for her younger sisters. Their care and comfort are often entrusted to her by her father. Further, Mari's father also relies on her to serve as his translator.

She helps him understand American customs and laws, particularly after his young brother Filipe has been arrested. Mari is further burdened with the complexities of the adult world when her mother's release is being negotiated. Her father confides in her, keeping her informed about what has happened, and her mother further explains to Mari much, but not all, of what has happened to her.

Similarly, Tyler is forced to confront the realities of the adult world as his father and mother contemplate the possible failure of the farm. Their decision to hire the Cruzes results ultimately in a situation in which Tyler and his family are complicit in a crime. Tyler reflects,

> if being a grown-up is this confusing,
> he wishes he could go back to that

happier country of childhood. But it's sort of sad how the minute you realize you've left it behind, you can never go back again.

As Tyler becomes increasingly involved in the Cruzes' lives, he feels compelled to help Mari and her family with their problems. Tyler takes on this burden in addition to the sense of duty he feels toward his own family. At the end of the novel, after Tyler and Mari have played significant roles in helping their parents with their own troubles, Tyler begins to understand what his mother has told him. In a letter to Mari, Tyler quotes his mother as saying, "When you're born as a child, you die as a baby. Just like when you're born as a teenager, you die as a child." Alvarez's portrayal of adolescence is one colored with darkness. Tyler and Mari both contend with the emotional pain and confusion involved in the development of their own friendship and in the evolution of their own roles within their families. The death Mrs. Paquette refers to, the journey from childhood toward adulthood, is depicted by Alvarez as a loss of innocence, a loss of a simple worldview in which children are protected from adult problems and the realities of an unjust world.

Third-Person Narration

Alvarez incorporates two distinct narrative styles within *Return to Sender*. Each chapter is divided into two sections. In one, Tyler's story is narrated in the present tense by a third-person narrator. In third-person narration, the character from whose point of view the story is told is referred to by his or her name, and by personal pronouns such as "he" or "she." (This is in contrast to a first-person narrator, who refers to himself or herself as "I.") Some third-person narrators are omniscient, that is, they are all-knowing and are able to reveal the thoughts and feelings of any character in the story. In Alvarez's novel, the author utilizes a third-person narrator with *limited* omniscience. Alvarez's narrator is limited to expressing only Tyler's thoughts and feelings. Tyler, in these sections of the novel, is the point-of-view character. He may wonder about the feelings of others, but any information the reader has regarding the other characters in the novel is based on Tyler's own observations or conversations other characters have that Tyler overhears. Using a third-person narrator whose omniscience is limited to Tyler alone, Alvarez allows the reader to establish a particular connection with Tyler. With the reader dependent on Tyler for information, Alvarez is able to present thoughts and feelings no one else sees and to provide the reader with a deep understanding of Tyler's character.

Epistolary Novel

The other narrative style Alvarez employs is that of the epistolary novel. An epistolary novel is one in which plot and character are revealed through letters written by one or more characters. In each chapter, after a section presented in Tyler's point of view, Mari reveals her own experience in the form of a letter. She reports on various events in the novel, such as what she is experiencing at school, or how the Paquettes are helping her jailed relatives, for example. As a letter writer, Mari uses first-person narration, referring to herself as "I." Alvarez's use of the epistolary form for Mari's sections of the novel allows the reader access to Mari's private thoughts, particularly when she is writing to her diary. Additionally, the intended recipients of Mari's letter reveal much about her character. She writes letters to her mother that will never be mailed, as she does not know her mother's whereabouts. She writes to Catholic saints, to the president of the United States, to her uncles, to her father, to her grandparents, to Tyler. These letters underscore Mari's values. She is a girl of faith who is idealistic enough to believe that one person can perhaps help change unfair laws. The letters further reveal that Mari's family is more important to her than anything else. She is determined to stay connected to them while they are separated, and this vigilance is transferred to Tyler as well after Mari is forced to leave the United States. As Mari indicates in a letter to Tyler, in which she suggests that the name of the farm be the "Stars and Swallows Farm," the connections she and her family have made to Tyler and his family, and to the United States in general, have changed her life and will continue to guide her. She feels that because she and Tyler can see the same stars, even when separated by thousands of miles, and that because the swallows make both the United States and Mexico their home, remaining connected, as she and Tyler will do with their letter writing, is both possible and extremely important.

Operation Return to Sender and Illegal Immigration

During President George W. Bush's administration (2001–2009), efforts were increased to deport illegal immigrants. A key component of Bush's immigration policy involved targeted raids on workplaces. In 2006, the Immigration and Customs Enforcement (ICE) agency initiated a series of raids on homes across the nation. One organized series of raids became known as Operation Return to Sender, in which the ICE agents targeted illegal aliens with criminal records. Reports indicate that over 2,100 individuals were arrested in Operation Return to Sender. However, as Nina Bernstein reports in a 2009 article for the *New York Times*, later investigations of ICE raids, such as Operation Return to Sender, indicated that a "vast majority of those arrested had no criminal record, and many had no deportation orders against them, either." Under the Obama administration, deportations of illegal workers has increased. In 2010, according Peter Slevin's *Washington Post* article, ICE estimated it would deport about 400,000 individuals, which was 10 percent above Bush's 2008 total. ICE director John Morton affirmed that the agency was focusing its efforts on criminals. Still, President Obama has been criticized for allowing many illegal immigrant criminals to remain free, and at the same time for targeting immigrants with no criminal records. Yet, according to ICE deportation statistics, deportation of convicted criminals has increased, from 195,772 individuals in the 2010 fiscal year to 216,698 in the 2011 fiscal year. Near the end of 2011, the Department of Homeland Security, in an effort to "allow severely overburdened immigration judges to focus on deporting foreigners who committed serious crimes or pose national risks," began reviewing deportation cases individually and initiated a training program for enforcement agents and lawyers, according to Julia Preston's 2011 article for the *New York Times*. In terms of the numbers of unauthorized immigrants from Mexico living in the United States, the Department of Homeland Security's Office of Immigration Statistics reported in 2012 that in 2011, 6,800,000 individuals from Mexico were residing illegally in the U.S.

Vermont Dairy Farming and Migrant Workers

In *Return to Sender*, Alvarez depicts the real-life plight of undocumented workers on Vermont's dairy farms. Often these farms are small family farms that are struggling financially. An organization designed to protect the rights of migrant laborers, Migrant Justice (formerly the Vermont Migrant Farmworker Solidarity Project) states that about 1,200 to 1,500 migrant workers "sustain Vermont's iconic dairy farms" and that these workers are employed by family dairy farms threatened "by deepening corporate control of agriculture." As the Migrant Justice organization points out, and as Alvarez's novel illustrates, both the migrant workers and the dairy farms are victims who are struggling to support their families. The Migrant Justice organization further reports that these migrant dairy workers are targets of "aggressive racial profiling practices that convert many workers into virtual prisoners on the farm." Vermont lawmakers are moving toward measures designed to alleviate this problem to some extent. In spring of 2012, a Vermont Senate bill passed that would allow Vermont residents, regardless of immigration status, access to state IDs and driver's licenses. This would allow immigrants greater mobility and a richer quality of life. Representative Diane Lanpher, quoted in an article by Andrea Suozzo for Vermont's *Addison County Independent*, expressed her surprise upon hearing what the workers have suffered. Suozzo states that Lanpher learned that workers were often unable to "access basic needs or medical help after being injured." Lanpher further pointed out that many seasonal industries have created programs for "guest workers" in which noncitizen immigrants can work legally in Vermont, yet no such federal program exists for dairy farm workers.

Critical Overview

Return to Sender was popular among critics upon its 2009 publication and garnered two major awards, the 2010 Americas Award for Children and Young Adult's Literature, and the American Library Association's Pura Belpré Award. Reviewers found much to praise. In an unsigned review for *Kirkus*, the critic describes the book as one that "effectively complicates simple equivalencies between what's illegal and what's wrong." The critic also finds praiseworthy Alvarez's "unhappily realistic conclusions," and describes the work as a "must-read." Still, the critic faulted the work, stating, "it lacks nuance" and is "unashamedly didactic." Sonja Bolle, a critic for the *Los Angeles Times*, points out that much of the current young-adult literature about the topic of immigration "tends to be earnest rather than artful." Bolle finds that Alvarez's work details adolescent struggles and notes that Alvarez "focuses on the children and their dawning comprehension of the complexities of the adult world." Bolle further maintains that although the work "is not as lively as Alvarez's other books," it "may be best read as a plea for treating neighbors like human beings." Maria Ferrer, in a review for *Hispanically Speaking News*, finds more to praise than criticize in the work, characterizing *Return to Sender* as "a wonderful, poignant, emotional book that will satisfy and engage all ages." Alice L. Trupe offers an in-depth examination of the novel's themes and structure in *Reading Julia Alvarez: The Pop Lit Book Club*, and observes that the "dual perspective" offered by the third-person portions of the book from Tyler's perspective and the letters written by Mari "shows Tyler's and Mari's growing understanding of each other as their families' fortunes intertwine."

What Do I Read Next?

- Alvarez's first novel, *How the García Girls Lost Their Accents*, published in 1991, relates the story of four sisters who immigrate to the United States with their parents in the 1960s. The work draws on Alvarez's own experiences and depicts the girls' upbringing by exploring the challenges they face in being tied to two distinct cultures— the Dominican culture of their parents and their new American culture.

- Alvarez's most recent work, the 2012 *A Wedding in Haiti: The Story of a Friendship*, tells the story of Alvarez's relationship with a young Haitian boy whom Alvarez met while establishing a farm and literacy organization in her native Dominican Republic. Years after the encounter, the child, now grown, asks Alvarez to come to his wedding in Haiti. The book chronicles Alvarez's experiences in Haiti as she travels to her friend's wedding.

- Guadalupe Garcia McCall's 2011 young-adult novel *Under the Mesquite* is told in free verse. The work captures the adolescence of a young girl born in Mexico and raised in the United States. The protagonist, Lupita, deals with issues of cultural and personal identity as she struggles to find her place in a large family and to cope with her mother's terminal illness.

- *Journeys Home: An Anthology of Contemporary African Diasporic Experience*, edited by Salome Nnoromele and Lisa Day-Lindsey, is a 2009 collection of poetry and personal narratives written by immigrants to the United States, the United Kingdom, and Europe from such locations as Ethiopia, Ghana, Liberia, Mali, and Uganda. The writers convey their experiences assimilating to the cultures of their new countries.

- Hirokazu Yoshikawa's 2011 book *Immigrants Raising Citizens: Undocumented Parents and Their Young Children* studies the experiences of individuals who have children while they are working in the United States as undocumented immigrants. Yoshikawa's work draws on data from a three-year study of nearly four hundred infants born to Dominican, Mexican, Chinese, and African American families.

- David Middleton's 2010 *Quite a Sightly Place: A Family Dairy Farm in Vermont* chronicles Middleton's four-year stint working on one of the few family-owned farms still in operation in Vermont. A photographer, Middleton captures images of daily life on the farm and details the farm's history and struggles.

Sources

"About Migrant Justice," in *Migrant Justice*, http://vtmfsp.org/about (accessed April 15, 2012).

Alvarez, Julia, "About Me," Julia Alvarez website, http://www.juliaalvarez.com/about (accessed April 15, 2012).

————, "Books," Julia Alvarez website, http://return-to-sender.juliaalvarez.com (accessed April 16, 2012).

————, *Return to Sender*, Yearling, 2009.

Bernstein, Nina, "Target of Immigrant Raids Shifted," in *New York Times*, February 4, 2009, http://www.nytimes.com/2009/02/04/us/04raids.htm (accessed April 15, 2012).

Bolle, Sonja, Review of *Return to Sender*, in *Los Angeles Times*, January 25, 2009, http://articles.latimes.com/2009/jan/25/entertainment julia-alvarez25 (accessed April 15, 2012).

Ferrer, Maria, Review of *Return to Sender*, in *Hispanically Speaking News*, November 21, 2010, http://www.hispanicallyspeakingnews.com/book-reviews/details/return-to-sender-by-juliaalvarez/3074/ (accessed April 15, 2012).

Hoefer, Michael, Nancy Rytina, and Bryan Baker, "Estimates of the Unauthorized Immigrant Population Residing in the United States: January 2011," in *Population Estimates*, Homeland Security

Office of Immigration Statistics, March 2012, http://www.dhs.gov/xlibrary/assets/statistics/publica (accessed April 15, 2012).

"ICE Removal Totals through February 20, 2012," U. S. Department of Homeland Security's Immigration and Customs Enforcement website, http://www.ice.gov/doclib/about/offices/ero/pdf/ero-removals1.pdf (accessed April 16, 2012).

Preston, Julia, "U.S. to Review Cases Seeking Deportations," in *New York Times*, November 17, 2011, http://www.nytimes.com/2011/11/17/us/deportation-cases-of-illegal-immigrants-to-be-reviewed.html (accessed April 16, 2012).

Review of *Return to Sender*, in *Kirkus Reviews*, November 15, 2008, https://www.kirkusreviews.com/book-reviews/juliaalvarez/return-to-sender-2/ (accessed April 15, 2012).

Review of *Return to Sender*, in *Publishers Weekly*, Vol. 255, No. 45, November 10, 2008, pp. 50–51.

Slevin, Peter, "Deportations of Illegal Immigrants Increases under Obama Administration," in *Washington Post*, July 26, 2010, http://www.washingtonpost.com/wp-dyn/content/article/2010/07/25/AR2010072501790.l (accessed April 15, 2012).

Suozzo, Andrea, "Migrant Driver's License Bill Advances in House," in *Addison County Independent*, April 12, 2012, http://www.addisonindependent.com/201204migrant drivers-license-bill-advances-house (accessed April 15, 2012).

Trupe, Alice L., "Books for Young Readers," in *Reading Julia Alvarez*, Greenwood Publishing, 2011, pp. 77–94.

Varnes, Kathrine, "Julia Alvarez," in *Dictionary of Literary Biography*, Vol. 282, *New Formalist Poets*, Thomson Gale, 2003, pp. 16–23.

Walker, Susan, "Julia Alvarez," in *Postcolonial Studies at Emory University*, Fall 1997, http://www.english.emory.edu/Bahri/Alvarez.html (accessed April 15, 2012).

"Wednesday, June 14," in *CNN World*, June 14, 2006, http://articles.cnn.com/2006-06-14/world/wednesday_1_homemade-bombs-tamil-tiger-rebels-twin-girls/3?_s=PM:WORLD (accessed April 15, 2012).

Further Reading

Blohm, Judith M., and Terri Lapinsky, *Kids Like Me: Voices of the Immigrant Experience*, Intercultural Press, 2006.

> Blohm and Lapinsky's work collects the personal narratives of immigrant children and discusses methods through which schoolchildren can begin to welcome and understand the immigrant students who enter their classrooms and communities.

Dvorak, William, ed., *Immigration in the United States*, H. W. Wilson, 2009.

> In this summary of twentieth-and twenty-first-century U.S. immigration policy, Dvorak offers an introduction to each section of the work, then compiles a collection of print resources dealing with each topic. He focuses on the changes in immigration policy throughout the twentieth century, discusses the challenges immigrants face upon entering the country, and highlights the efforts of the United States to keep illegal immigrants from crossing the U.S.-Mexican border.

Llana, Sara Miller, "Home Again in Mexico: Illegal

Immigration Hits Net Zero," in *Christian Science Monitor Weekly*, April 8, 2012, http://www.csmonitor.com/World/Americas/2012/04 again-in-Mexico-Illegal-immigration-hits-net-zero (accessed April 15, 2012).

> Llana's article describes the lives and motivations of Mexican citizens who have returned to Mexico after living as illegal immigrants in the United States.

Maroney, James H., *The Political Economy of Milk: Reinvigorating Vermont's Family Dairy Farms*, Gala Books, 2009.

> Maroney explores the history of the Vermont dairy farming industry from the administration of Calvin Coolidge through the present day, spotlighting aspects of regulation and consolidation that have resulted in the current difficulties the industry faces.

Suggested Search Terms

Julia Alvarez AND Return to Sender Julia Alvarez AND illegal immigration Julia Alvarez AND Vermont dairy farming Julia Alvarez AND young-adult fiction Julia Alvarez AND Operation Return to Sender Julia Alvarez AND epistolary novel Julia Alvarez AND poetry

Julia Alvarez AND Dominican Republic Julia Alvarez AND Spanish writings Julia Alvarez AND immigration reform